SPECIAL
CEREMONIES

Pilgrimages and Journeys

Cath Senker

SPECIAL
CEREMONIES
Pilgrimages and Journeys

This book is based on the original title *Pilgrimages and Journeys* by Sue Kendall, in the *Ceremonies and Celebrations* series, published in 2000 by Hodder Wayland.

This differentiated text version is by Cath Senker, published in Great Britain in 2005 by Hodder Wayland, an imprint of Hodder Children's Books.

This paperback edition published in 2006 by Wayland, an imprint of Hachette Children's Books.

© Copyright 2005 Wayland

Original designer: Tim Mayer
Layout for this edition: Jane Hawkins

Consultants:
Working Group on Sikhs and Education (WORKSE);
Rasamandala Das;
Jane Clements, The Council of Christians and Jews;
Jonathan Gorsky, The Council of Christians and Jews;
Dr Fatma Amer, London Central Mosque;
The Clear Vision Trust.

The right of Cath Senker to be indentified as the author of this Work has been asserted by her in accordance with the Copyright, Designs and Patents Act 1988

Wayland
An imprint of Hachette Children's Books
338 Euston Road, London NW1 3BH

All possible care has been taken to trace ownership of each photograph in the book and to obtain copyright permission for its use. If there are any omissions or if any errors have occured they will be corrected in subsequent editions, on notification to the publishers.

Picture acknowledgements:
Circa Picture Library 13, 17 (Robyn Beeche), Hutchison Library 5 (J. Horner), 8 (B. Regent), 25; Peter Sanders 19, 20, 21; Tony Stone Images 6 (Louis Grandadam), 10 (Paul Chesley), 16 (David Sutherland); Trip 1 (A. Tovy), 4, 7 (M. Both), 9 (Z. Harasym), 11 (H. Isachar), 12 (A. Tovy), 14 (Dinodia), 15 (Resource Foto), 18, 22 (Dinodia), 23 (J. Sweeney), 24 (H. Rogers), 26 (H. Rogers), 27 (H. Rogers), 28 (H. Rogers), 29 (H. Rogers).

British Library Cataloguing in Publication Data
Senker, Cath
Pilgrimages and journeys. - Differentiated ed. - (Special ceremonies)
1.Pilgrims and pilgrimages - Juvenile literature
I.Title II.Kendall, Sue
203.5'1

ISBN-10: 0 7502 4975 7
ISBN-13: 978 0 7502 4975 1

Contents

What is a Pilgrimage?

People all over the world have places that are special to them. Perhaps they remind them of a particular person or event. They could be places that help them to strengthen their religious beliefs.

It is often part of the religious tradition to visit these sites. This kind of visit is called a 'pilgrimage'. People may travel alone or with a group. They may go once during their life, or regularly.

◄ These Muslims are in Makkah for the *hajj* (pilgrimage).

A special time

On pilgrimage, people perform rituals
and worship together. Some may pray and
meditate alone. Many pilgrims save up for
years for their journey and greatly look
forward to this special time. This book
introduces you to pilgrimages made by
people of the six major religions.

▲ The Western Wall in
Jerusalem is a place of
pilgrimage for Jewish
people.

The Christian Tradition

▲ The Pope blesses the crowd in Rome, Italy.

Christians believe that God sent his son, Jesus, into the world to show people how to live good lives. Many Christians like to visit the places that were important in Jesus' life. Others go to places where they believe miracles happened.

Going on a pilgrimage helps people to refresh their faith. They may thank God for good things that have happened, or ask forgiveness for wrong deeds. Pilgrimages can be at any time of year but many people go at festival times.

The Pope

Many Roman Catholic Christians travel to Rome, Italy to hear the Pope's teachings. They believe God chose the Pope to lead the Church.

SOPHIE'S STORY

'Last Easter, I went on a pilgrimage to Jerusalem with my mum. We went to the Old City. There were thousands of people walking really slowly behind men carrying a heavy wooden cross – like Jesus did on his own. People in the procession were praying quietly and singing hymns. It felt very special to walk where Jesus had walked.'

▲ These pilgrims carry a cross in the Good Friday procession in Jerusalem.

The Holy Land

Many Christians try to go to the Holy Land to visit the places where they believe Jesus lived. In Jerusalem, they can see where the Romans led him to his death. They can also see where people think he was buried. It is said that Jesus rose from the dead on Easter Day.

Easter is a very important festival. On Good Friday, many pilgrims join the procession in Jerusalem. They remember the events that led to Jesus' death, and pray.

▲ These pilgrims in Lourdes, France are at a healing ceremony. They hope to be cured of their illnesses.

Miracles

All over the world there are places where people believe miracles have happened. Christians make journeys to these sites to pray for people who are ill or suffering. They ask God to cure them.

Many Christians believe the Virgin Mary appeared to a young girl in Lourdes, France in 1858. She told her where to find a source of healing water. Pilgrims go to Lourdes for healing ceremonies or to fetch holy water.

These worshippers in Poland are carrying a statue of the Virgin Mary. ▼

SACRED TEXT ✝

Jesus and his parents went on pilgrimage to Jerusalem for Passover. Twelve-year-old Jesus stayed to talk to wise men. 'And when they had fulfilled the days, as they returned, the child Jesus tarried [stayed] behind in Jerusalem and Joseph [Jesus' earthly father] and his mother knew not of it. And it came to pass, that after three days they found him in the temple, sitting in the midst of the doctors, both hearing them and asking them questions.'

The Bible: Luke 2:41-47

The Jewish Tradition

Jews believe that God rescued their people from Egypt about 3,000 years ago. He gave them the Promised Land, then called Canaan. During the twentieth century, Jewish people founded the State of Israel on that land. Many Jews visit Israel to remember the great events in their history.

The Western Wall

Jerusalem is at the heart of the Jewish religion. The Western Wall in the Old City is the only remaining part of the Jewish Temple, which was destroyed in 70 CE. Many worshippers gather there to pray. Men and women worship separately. Some visitors write personal prayers on small pieces of paper and push them into the cracks between the stones.

◀ This Jewish man is praying at the Western Wall.

SACRED TEXT

This is part of a prayer that Jews say before going on a journey.

'O deliver us from every enemy, ambush and hurt by the way, and from all afflictions [troubles] that visit and trouble the world.'

From the *Authorized Daily Prayer Book*

Before the destruction of their Temple, Jewish people flocked to it on the holidays of *Pesach*, *Shavuot* and *Sukkot*. These are known as the Pilgrim Festivals. Nowadays, there are no fixed times for pilgrimages. But some people in Jerusalem choose to visit the ruins during the main festivals, such as *Pesach*.

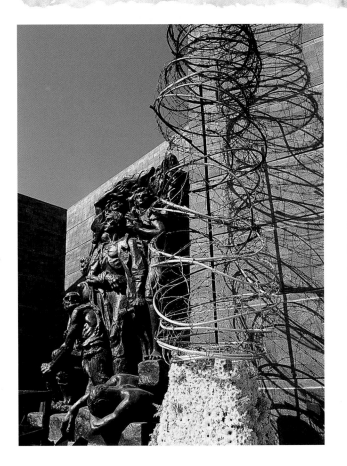

The Holocaust

Some people make a special visit to Yad Vashem. This is a memorial in Israel, a special place built to remember all the Jewish people who were killed or harmed during the Holocaust in the 1940s. When they visit, some people say prayers or light candles for the dead.

◄ This is a memorial at Yad Vashem showing Jewish people fighting the Nazis in Poland.

The *kibbutz*

A *kibbutz* is a community in Israel that is owned by all its members. Most *kibbutz* members work within the community in agriculture, industry and shared areas such as the dining hall. Young volunteers from around the world are welcome to visit or live and work on a *kibbutz* for a few months. Many Jewish people do this to deepen their understanding of what it means to be a Jew.

This woman is gathering strawberries on a *kibbutz.* ▼

Pesach

At *Pesach*, many Jewish people around the world remember the journey their people made in ancient times to escape the cruel rule of the Egyptians. Families gather for the *Seder*, a special service. They read the story of the journey, enjoy a special meal and sing songs.

▲ The foods on this special *Seder* plate are used during the service as symbols of how God looked after the Jewish people.

BEN'S STORY

'I'm 12 and I live in Leeds. Last year our family travelled to Israel. I felt honoured to go to the Western Wall. Dad and I said prayers side by side, and I wrote a prayer for my sick grandma. Going to Israel helped me to remember our Jewish history.'

The Hindu Tradition

Hindus worship different forms of God, often depending on which part of India their family originally came from. If they choose to make a *yatra*, or pilgrimage, they often go to a place that is connected to a particular deity (god or goddess). Some Hindus consider it a duty to go on a pilgrimage to win God's favour and blessings.

At the annual *Ratha Yatra* festival, giant *murtis* (sacred statues) of Lord Krishna and his brother and sister are pulled through the streets in huge chariots. ▼

▲ These actors are dressed as Rama and Sita in a performance of the *Ramayana*.

Places of pilgrimage

There are many holy places in India. The most popular is Varanasi, on the River Ganges. Its main temple is dedicated to Shiva. Another deity, Krishna, lived in the sacred village of Vrindavan, and is worshipped during the *Ratha Yatra* festival in Puri. At Rameshvaram, in the south, worshippers of Rama watch plays of the *Ramayana* – the long Hindu poem about Rama's adventures.

SACRED TEXT

This text tells Hindus that going on pilgrimages is a good way of praising God.

'O my friend, please, therefore, chant the glories of the Lord, who is meant to be glorified in the places of pilgrimage.'

From *the Bhagavat Purana 3.1.45*

15

Holy rivers

Hindus often make pilgrimages to important rivers and water sources. Many people try to visit the River Ganges in India. They bathe in its holy waters, which they believe will purify them. Some walk barefoot, out of devotion and to show respect to holy ground.

When a Hindu dies, the body is cremated (burnt). Hindus believe that burning the body allows the soul to move on to its next life. Then the ashes of the person are scattered over the River Ganges if possible.

These worshippers are bathing in the holy River Ganges in Varanasi. ▼

ASHVIN'S STORY

'I'm nearly eleven and I live in New York. Last year my grandad died. I travelled with my parents, sisters and grandma to India. We went to Varanasi and bathed in the River Ganges. Then dad scattered grandad's ashes over the water.'

On *yatra*

Many people decide to make a pilgrimage (yatra) just before an important event, such as a wedding. They believe it brings good luck. At the pilgrimage site, Hindus meditate and worship the local deities. They make offerings (gifts to the gods) and perform a ceremony with lighted candles to show their devotion. *Yatra* is a joyful time.

These pilgrims are visiting Vrindavan, the place where Hindus believe Lord Krishna lived as a child. ▶

The Muslim Tradition

For many Muslims, the greatest way to strengthen their faith is to go on *hajj*, the pilgrimage to the holy city of Makkah in Saudi Arabia.

Hajj

Muslims believe it was in Makkah that the Prophet Muhammad ﷺ received messages from Allah. One of their duties as Muslims is to go on *hajj* at least once in their lifetime. Only Muslims are allowed into Makkah.

Here, Muslim men and women gather at the start of the pilgrimage. ▼

▲ These Muslims are circling the *Ka'bah* in Makkah.

Every year, millions of Muslims from all over the world go on *hajj*. It always takes place at the same time in the Muslim year, although it varies in the Western calendar. *Hajj* is an exciting time when Muslims from all over the world gather together. All pilgrims wear simple white clothes to show that everyone is equal before Allah.

SACRED TEXT

This tells how Allah called people to Makkah:

'And proclaim unto mankind the pilgrimage. They will come unto thee on foot and on every lean camel...'

Qur'an: XXII 27

▲ This woman drinks from the well of Zamzam.

Rituals of *hajj*

Many *hajj* rituals help people to remember the experiences of the Prophet Ibrahim ﷺ, his wife Hagar and son Isma'il.

When Muslims pray, they always face towards the *Ka'bah* in Makkah, the first monument built on Earth for the worship of Allah. On *hajj*, everyone circles the *Ka'bah* seven times. Next, they run between the two hills of Safa and Marwah as Hagar did, in search of water. They drink from the well of Zamzam, where water appeared for Hagar in a miracle.

The pilgrims go to Mount Arafat, where the Prophet ﷺ gave his last sermon. Then they travel to Muzdalifah. There they spend all night praying and reading the *Qur'an*, their holy book. The following day, they throw stones at the three pillars at Jamarat, which stand for the devil.

The final day is the Feast of *Id ul-Adha*. Muslims remember how Ibrahim ﷺ was prepared to kill his son in obedience of Allah's will. Going on *hajj* is tiring yet it strengthens Muslims' faith.

These pilgrims are throwing stones at the pillars of Jamarat. ▼

DANAH'S STORY

'I'm eleven years old. This year my brother and dad went on *hajj*. They brought me and mum some holy water from the well of Zamzam. Dad has carefully folded the clothes he wore on *hajj*. He says he wants to keep them for ever.'

The Buddhist Tradition

Buddhists follow the teachings of the Buddha. Born a wealthy prince 2,500 years ago, he left his palace to find out the causes of suffering and how to escape from it. He eventually found the answer and became the Buddha, the Enlightened One – 'one who understands how life really is'.

The Buddha taught that if people want to suffer less they need to train themselves to be kinder and wiser and to tell the truth.

The Buddha taught that people should meditate, sitting quietly and still, in order to become calm and develop wisdom.

▲ This picture shows the Buddha in meditation.

◄ Pilgrims have decorated this tree in Bodh Gaya. They believe the Buddha sat underneath it.

The journey through life

Buddhists think of life as a journey. They may also travel to places important to Buddhism to help them to develop their beliefs. They go to Lumbini, Nepal, where the Buddha was born. Bodh Gaya, India, is where he became Enlightened. At Sarnath, India the Buddha gave his first teachings, and Kushinagar, India is where he died.

SACRED TEXT

Here the Buddha tells his disciple, Ananda, about pilgrimages.

'...there are four places that should make the faithful happy: the place where I was born (Lumbini); the place where I gained Enlightenment (Body Gaya); the place where I first taught the way out of suffering (Sarnath) and the place where I will die (Kushinagar)."

Adapted from the Digha Nikaya: *Maha Parinibbana Sutta*

Temples and sacred buildings

Worshippers might not be able to travel to far-away holy places. They may visit temples and *stupas* (sacred monuments) nearer home. There they listen to teachings, join in worship, meditate and make offerings of flowers, gifts and incense. These activities help them to keep their enthusiasm for following the Buddhist path in life.

These monks are praying in Sarnath, where the Buddha gave his first teachings. ▼

Wesak

Buddhists may go on a pilgrimage at any time, but many choose to go during a Buddhist festival. They meet other followers and think about how to develop their beliefs.

Wesak (in May or June) is an important Buddhist festival and a good time for visiting special places. At *Wesak*, Buddhists remember the Buddha's birth, Enlightenment and death. Pilgrimage sites are usually decorated for the occasion.

People from other religions also like to visit Buddhist shrines and temples to listen to the Buddha's teachings.

These pilgrims are visiting the *stupa* in Sarnath. ▶

IAN'S STORY

'I live in Holland and my family is Buddhist. Recently, a group from my temple went to Lumbini, where the Buddha was born. We walked up the hill to the monastery to hear the monks' teaching. The statues of the Buddha were beautiful. I laid an offering of a bunch of bright flowers at the Buddha's feet.'

The Sikh Tradition

Guru Nanak started the Sikh religion about five hundred years ago in the Punjab, India. He believed that there was a new way to serve God by praying, working hard and helping people. Guru Nanak was the first of ten Sikh Gurus.

The Golden Temple

Many Sikhs like to visit the sites of important events in the Gurus' lives. A very special place is the Golden Temple at Amritsar in India.

This is the magnificent Golden Temple. ▼

It is ritual to bathe in the lake around the Golden Temple.

SACRED TEXT

This text from the Sikh holy book describes how Sikhs should devote themselves to God.

'The souls on their spiritual journey chant and meditate within their minds on the One Lord, the Treasure of Excellence.'

From the *Guru Granth Sahib*

The fifth Guru, Arjan Dev, built the Golden Temple. It has four entrances facing in all four directions. This shows that Sikhs welcome people from all parts of the world. They believe that all people are equal.

▲ Worshippers at the Golden Temple share the *langar* meal from leaf plates.

Sikh worship

Inside the Golden Temple, Sikhs listen to the *granthi* (reader) reciting from the *Guru Granth Sahib*. They join in with prayers and sing hymns. After worship, everyone enjoys a shared meal, called *langar*. It is provided free to all visitors to the temple. Sharing food together shows that everyone is equal.

BANDHA'S STORY

'I'm ten years old and I live in Ireland. My family is going to Amritsar this April. I'm looking forward to meeting Sikhs from around the world and sharing *langar* with thousands of people. I know it will make me feel proud to be Sikh.'

Festival pilgrimages

There is no set time for pilgrimages but Sikhs often go at festival times, such as the birthdays of the Gurus. *Baisakhi* is the main festival, and the busiest time to go. On this holiday, Sikhs remember the founding of their community by Guru Gobind Singh. Many choose to be baptized into the faith at this time.

Going on a journey to a holy site is a special time and is enjoyable too. Sikhs can share their experiences with people from all over the world. It is also a private time, when they can strengthen their personal faith.

These pilgrims place flowers at the Golden Temple. ▼

Glossary

baptize to welcome somebody into the Church, usually by pouring a few drops of water on to the person's head.

CE the Christian Era (also called the Common Era), dating from the death of Jesus.

disciple follower.

Guru (Sikh and Buddhist) teacher.

Holy Land the name Christians use for the land that is now Israel and Palestine.

incense a substance that is burned to give off a pleasant smell.

Krishna, Lord a Hindu deity; a form of Vishnu who came down to Earth to overcome evil.

meditate to sit quietly and still to help you become calm, happy and wise.

memorial a statue or building to remind people of an important event or a famous person who has died.

miracle a special event that it is believed was caused by God.

offerings food, flowers or other gifts that are offered to a statue of the Buddha to thank him for his teachings.

Rama, Prince the hero of the *Ramayana*. A Hindu form of God who came to Earth.

ritual a series of actions that are always carried out in the same way as part of a religious ceremony.

Roman Catholic a member of the Catholic Church, which is led by the Pope in Rome, Italy.

sermon a talk about a religious topic.

soul the special part of a person that makes them who they are. People of some religions believe their soul will be reborn in another body after they have died.

tomb a large grave.

Virgin Mary the mother of Jesus.

Books to Read

Beliefs and Cultures: Buddhist; Christian; Hindu; Jewish; Muslim, (Watts, 2003.)

Festivals of the World by Elizabeth Breuilly, Joanne O'Brien and Martin Palmer, (Hodder Wayland, 2002.)

Our Culture: Buddhist; Hindu; Jewish; Muslim; Sikh, (Watts, 2003.)

The Facts About Buddhism; Sikhism; Judaism; Christianity; Hinduism; Islam by Alison Cooper (Hodder Wayland, 2006)

A Year of Religious Festivals series: *My Buddhist Year; My Christian Year; My Hindu Year; My Jewish Year; My Muslim Year; My Sikh Year* by Cath Senker (Hodder Wayland, 2004/2005)

Index

All the numbers in **bold** refer to photographs